D0536072

Fur

by Jennifer Boothroyd

first step nonfiction

Lerner Publications Company · Minneapolis

Cats, dogs, and people are
animals called **mammals**.

Mammals have **fur** or hair
on top of their **skin**.

3

Lions have a lot of fur.

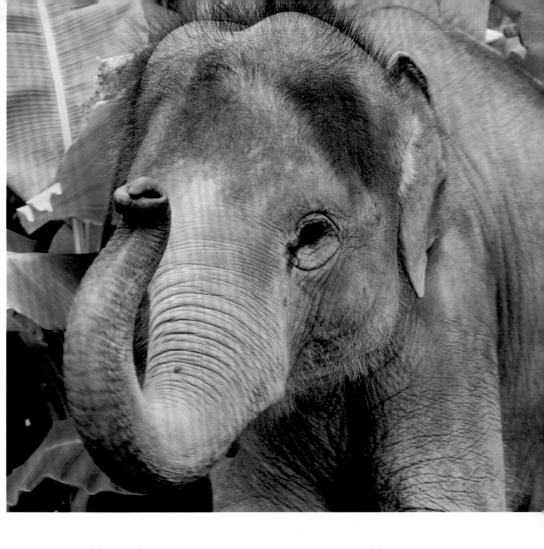

Elephants have a little fur.

Some fur is soft.

Some hair is long.

Many animals have hair in
their ears and near their eyes.

This hair keeps out dirt
and bugs.

Fur keeps an animal's
skin dry.

Fur can be different colors.

Animal fur can change.

This bunny grows white fur
in the winter.

Fur helps animals hide. This
is called **camouflage**.

A fawn looks different from
its mother.

Animals **shed** their old fur.

Fur helps animals in their
surroundings.

Mammals Are Everywhere

Fur helps mammals live all over the world. Leopard seals and beavers have thick waterproof fur. It helps them stay warm. Hedgehogs have spiny fur. It protects them from hunting animals. A gorilla's hair protects it from insect bites. A giant anteater has a fluffy tail. In cold weather, it uses its tail like a blanket. A panda has a thick coat. The coat keeps it warm in the cold mountains. A wallaby's fur makes it hard to see.

Furry Animals around the World

beaver

hedgehog

panda

EUROPE

ASIA

NORTH
AMERICA

SOUTH
AMERICA

AFRICA

AUSTRALIA

giant
anteater

gorilla

wallaby

leopard
seal

ANTARCTICA

Facts about Fur

 Hair and fur are made of keratin. Fish scales and fingernails are made of the same material.

 Porcupine quills are stiff, sharp hairs. They protect the porcupine from hunting animals.

 Whales and dolphins are born with hair. They lose their hair as they grow.

 Green alga is a plant. It can grow in the fur of a sloth.

 Tiny muscles make your hairs stand up when you get cold.

 Humans shave off hair from sheep and llamas. This hair is called wool. Wool grows back.

 Seals have short, thick fur. It protects their skin from sharp rocks.

 Lynx have long hairs on their feet. This fur helps them move in the snow.

Glossary

 camouflage – coloring that makes an animal look like its surroundings

 fur – the hairy coat of some mammals

 mammals – warm-blooded animals with hair or fur that drink their mother's milk

 shed – to lose or fall off

 skin – the outer covering of a person or animal

Index

The images in this book are used with the permission of: © Shalom Ormsby/Blend Images/Getty Images, pp. 2, 22 (third from top); © Frans Lemmens/SuperStock, pp. 3, 22 (second from top); © Nstanev/Dreamstime.com, p. 4; © Gerry Ellis/Minden Pictures, pp. 5, 22 (bottom); © GK Hart/Vicki Hart/Stone/Getty Images, p. 6; © Bandit/Dreamstime.com, p. 7; © Clara/Shutterstock Images, p. 8; © Martin Child/Digital Vision/Getty Images, p. 9; © Neelsky/Shutterstock Images, p. 10; © Anan Kaewkhammul/Shutterstock Images, p. 11; © Rich Reid/National Geographic/Getty Images, p. 12; © Thorsten Milse/Robert Harding World Imagery/Corbis, p. 13; © Joel Sartore/National Geographic/Getty Images, pp. 14, 22 (top); © Gsagi13/Dreamstime.com, p. 15; © Dynamic Light USA/Alamy, pp. 16, 22 (fourth from top); © Igorj/Dreamstime.com, p. 17; © Francocogoli/Dreamstime.com, p. 19 (top/left); © Christopher Moncrieff/Dreamstime.com, p. 19 (top/middle), 19 (bottom/right); © John Giustina/Taxi/Getty Images, p. 19 (top/right); © Nestor Noci/Shutterstock Images, p. 19 (middle/left); © Surz01/Dreamstime.com, p. 19 (middle/center); © Derek Rogers/Dreamstime.com, p. 19 (bottom). Front Cover: © Vita Khorzhevska/Shutterstock Images.

Main body text set in ITC Avant Garde Gothic 21/25. Typeface provided by Adobe Systems.

Lerner Publications Company
A division of Lerner Publishing Group, Inc.
241 First Avenue North
Minneapolis, MN 55401 U.S.A.

Website address: www.lernerbooks.com

Library of Congress Cataloging-in-Publication Data

Boothroyd, Jennifer, 1972-
    Fur / by Jennifer Boothroyd.
       p.   cm. — (First step nonfiction — Body coverings)
    Includes index.
    ISBN 978-0-7613-5786-5 (lib. bdg. : alk. paper)
    1. Fur—Juvenile literature. I. Title.
    QL942.B66 2012
    599.7'147—dc22   2010050649

Manufactured in the United States of America
1 – PC – 7/15/11